No Thanks, I'm Good

Saying No to Anxiety and Reclaiming Your Power

Maria Sarnatora

Published by TSH Publishing Company, LLC

TABLE OF CONTENTS

DEDICATION

I dedicate this book to my son, whose entrance into this world changed me, motivated me to be someone who refuses to play small, and whose love inspires me every day. To my husband, who has the patience of a saint and supports me every step of the way. And to my fur babies, who bring joy to my life on the regular.

"You only have control over three things in your life—the thoughts you think, the images you visualize, and the actions you take."

JACK CANFIELD

INTRO

I used to think that everyone experienced the same type of thoughts that I did. I assumed what went through my head was just common sense until one day I grew to understand that it's a type of anxiety, and that this neuroticism I experience daily is, in fact, not shared by everyone. Inevitably, after I realized this, I felt like I was some crazy freak and it caused me to develop a deep sense of distrust of my mind until more recent years. The interesting thing is, the type of anxiety I experienced seemed quite normal in my house growing up, and in fact was encouraged. As I grew older, I realized that not everyone worried as much as I did. I blew it off and termed it "street smarts" handed down to me by two parents who grew up in the city, but now that I think back, it looked and felt a lot more like high functioning anxiety.

I'm not talking about the kind of anxiety that would prevent you from doing everyday tasks such as leaving your house or socializing with others. The type I experience every day doesn't impact my daily functioning to where it's noticeable. In fact, I went through all of graduate school and came out with a degree in mental health without knowing anything about high functioning anxiety. Because I was so focused on all the formal well-known mental health diagnoses and all of their specific criteria, I didn't realize that I'd been walking around with a very real issue. High functioning anxiety doesn't exist in the textbooks because it's not a recognized mental health diagnosis. I also realized only in the past few years that so many other people are walking around with this or experiencing something similar. I am most definitely not alone…and so if you also identify as someone with high functioning anxiety, you, my friend, are not alone either.

My anxiety started in childhood but didn't exacerbate until college, when I started having panic attacks. I would get them randomly, in my dorm or during class, for what seemed like no particular reason. However, now as I look back, I know I had been experiencing a lot of stress at the time. Stress that I had been ignoring until finally, my body said enough is enough. I started therapy soon after and continued to utilize therapy to work through all I had been going through for a number of years, and so because of that, they became less frequent. It wasn't until many years later that they crept up again. However, this time around, I learned that I have more control over them than I initially thought.

I was driving to work one day back in the winter of 2017. I was only a few minutes away from the office out of an hour and 15 minute drive and out of nowhere, I suddenly felt like I couldn't breathe. It felt like I was suffocating. The blood had rushed to my neck area, and I felt as though if I didn't pull the clothing I had on away from my skin; I was going to pass out. I immediately unzipped my jacket and pulled my shirt away from my neck to feel like I could breathe again. I knew what this was because it wasn't the first time this happened to me. I assured myself it was just a panic attack. I'd become so familiar with these over the years since college that I knew I wouldn't die. I also knew that if I didn't calm myself down and keep my focus on the road, I could easily get into a car accident. Once I felt like I could breathe again, I tried to ignore the feeling of the world closing in on me until I parked the car at my office building. When I entered the building, I ran straight to my supervisor's office and broke down. Luckily, I worked in an office filled with therapists and my supervisor at the time was a very good one. I felt comfortable enough to confide in her, and she held the space I needed for this. She knew what I had been experiencing the past several weeks, so it probably wasn't a huge surprise to find me in a state of distress. For the last few weeks prior to this event, I had been having some weird health issues. I had this ongoing feeling that there was something caught in my throat, down at the top of my chest and no matter what I did, it wouldn't go away. I finally went to go see a gastroenterologist and eventually had some testing done, only to find that there was nothing and the doctor could not come up with a reason for the discomfort. It left me in a state of wondering and worrying about this unknown reason.

After recuperating from my morning breakdown, when I finally returned home that day, I prayed to God to help me figure out what to do because I needed an answer to what was going on with me. Well, God answered extremely fast because the next thing I knew, as I was scrolling through Pinterest, a pin popped up that caught my eye. It was a picture of the universe in the shape of a human being gently holding the head of another woman next to her saying," I got you, just control your mind." Now, this might not seem like much of a sign, but I knew without a doubt, as soon as I saw it that this was a message for me. Tears flooded my eyes because at that moment I realized God answered my prayer and was telling me I was OK. HE sent me a sign telling me what I needed to understand. That it was all in my head and that I had control of this if I could just control my brain. I then thought about how I could feel more in control of my mind and the first thing that popped up was meditation. Now, I'm not a meditator and when I say that, it's not because I don't like it or don't believe in it. I struggle to keep my head quiet and if I am successful with it, I usually end up falling asleep, but I knew this was a way to control one's mind, so I decided to try. I looked up a guided meditation on YouTube and let myself be calm while I listened. Once the meditation was complete, I felt a little better and believe it or not, by the next morning, the feeling in my throat was completely gone! I was so excited that my prayer was answered. I had asked

God, noticed HIS sign, listened to it... and it worked!

For a few months or so leading up to this day, I had been struggling and unhappy at work. I liked my company, but my role within the organization combined with the lack of self-care I provided myself left me feeling like I was taking on the weight of the world every day. Looking back, I had been internalizing so much that my body just couldn't handle it anymore. In fact, my entire career I had felt that way but never admitted it to myself. After years of internalizing, I reached my breaking point. I was completely out of alignment and it manifested in my body, specifically in my throat until the day it magically disappeared.

Now, I wish I could tell you this was the end of my anxiety, but it wasn't. In fact, this experience, as eye-opening as it was, led me to think that I couldn't trust what was going on inside my own head. I disliked myself because of it and felt like I was at war with a part of my brain therefore I shouldn't listen to what I feel or think because I can't trust it. In reality all I needed to do was to differentiate my intuition from ego, but I didn't learn this until years later. I continued on for years, double thinking my every decision, double thinking other people's decisions, and pretty much living in a world of catastrophic thinking. Catastrophic thinking is when your mind goes to the very worst thing that could happen at any moment. I would then make decisions based on the fear of that thought happening and how I could avoid it.

For example, if I needed my mom to run to the store for me, immediately I would start to worry that something would happen to her while on her way there. Because I wouldn't be able to live with myself for being the reason something like that happened to her, I wouldn't ask her to help me at all. Want to stress yourself out 24/7? Adopt catastrophic thinking... no seriously, don't.

I suppose now you want me to get to the point of the story where I learned how to get rid of my anxiety and catastrophic thinking for good and as much as I'd love to share that part with you, I can't. The reason for that is because it hasn't happened. I still have high functioning anxiety and my mind still goes to the worst, BUT the difference now is that I have learned to control it. I have learned to decipher when my intuition is speaking to me and when my ego is (we'll get into that later) and I've learned how to have better control of what I allow myself to focus on. But for the first time in what seems like forever... I feel so much freedom from something that felt so inhibiting in the past.

If you're someone who is now convincing themselves that this book won't be of help to you because you've never experienced a panic attack before, you're wrong. This book is for those who experience panic attacks, high functioning anxiety, and also for those with limiting beliefs, low confidence, and perfectionism. It is basically for anyone who has ever worried about anything at all in their life. If that's you, I can assure you that you will relate in some way shape or form and find a takeaway that will hopefully improve the quality of your everyday life.

My goal in writing this book is to help you understand what is going on in your head, accept yourself for who you are (anxiety and all), and help you see how you can regain control. In doing so you will be able to free yourself from what weighs you down in order to live your life to the fullest. Why, you ask? Because life's too short and too damn precious for us to be sitting around all worried and stuck in fear. The time we have here on earth is too great to be letting your fears dictate your life. You are too amazing to be depriving yourself just because you worry about the outcome. I'm not saying be reckless, but I am saying live. I can tell you right now that far too many people out there are not fully living their lives without even realizing it, because their fears are controlling them.

How will you get value from this book? Read it with an open mind. My educational and professional background is a beautiful mix of Mental Health Counseling (which is what my degree is in), Client Services, Training, and Coaching. Despite my background, I am not writing this as a mental health therapist, and I am not writing this as a coach. You will not find a bunch of research or science backed theories explained in this book, nor will you find any clinical jargon. The reason for this is not because I don't find it valuable because I do, but because I experience anxiety as a regular human being and I've learned how to manage it through the lens of a regular human being. I may be familiar with therapeutic interventions, but I can assure you I didn't sit there and try to treat myself with them. I was never a therapist in my journey with anxiety, but always the client. I learned through experience and using that experience, I now coach myself through it. I'm here as a person who wants to share what she has learned with the world in hopes it will help others as well. I do not take credit for any of these ideas. I've simply taken what I've learned that has helped me over the past several years, whether it be from my experience in therapy, as a coaching client, and as a human being just trying to live a full life, and have put it all together for you in one place. I'm also still learning, every day. As a recovering perfectionist, I acknowledge this book is not perfect, and yet I wrote it despite the nagging fear in my brain. In doing this I'm accepting imperfection, being vulnerable, and putting it out there anyway. My heart tells me this can help someone, perhaps change a life for the better and that alone is enough to fight through my fear. I encourage you to give it a chance. Try it out for yourself and see what aligns best with you. My hope is to be one tiny, but bright light that helps you see the way to becoming the best version of yourself and saying, "No thanks, I'm good" to your fears, anxiety, and any other bullshit that doesn't serve you. Now let's do this...

"Awareness is like the sun. When it shines on things, they are transformed."

THICH NHAT HANH

CHAPTER 1
THE KEY

"Do you want to know how many times you said umm?" My old manager asked after listening to me present for one of the first times to one of our customer companies. "Not really, but OK tell me," I replied, wincing, in preparation, for the answer. Now in all honesty, I can't remember what the number was, probably because I blocked it from my memory, but I'll never forget how surprised I was at how often it crept in, especially because I was relatively confident about the subject matter. All she had to do was make me aware of just how often I was saying it and from then on I was hyper vigilant about letting it slip. The next time I presented, I asked her afterwards to tell me how many times I said, "Umm." Do you know what she told me? She replied "Not enough for me to keep track." Now that doesn't mean that I don't let an "umm" slip every once in a while, but my awareness of it helped me change this unwanted habit. It allowed me to slow down and gave me time to stop and think before it had a chance to escape my lips, so I could replace it with a better word.

I think the most important step with anything you are trying to change is awareness. We go about life so fast, sometimes too fast to think as clearly as we'd like and take notice of our behaviors. Therefore, if we don't know we are doing something unfavorable, we cannot choose differently. This is what makes awareness the key that unlocks the door to change.

The first step in the process of awareness for managing our anxiety is to let the fact sink in that you are not powerless. I'll say it again because it needs to be repeated: You are not powerless. You have the ability, whether you realize it or not, to help your situation. I'm not saying you are to blame for having your anxiety in the first place because I don't believe that at all. You have a choice though, to either let it control you, or take the steps you need to reclaim control and take your power back. Let that sink in. If you only take away one thing from this book, even though I doubt that would be the case, my hope is it would be this: You have more control than you think.

The second step in this process of awareness is trickier. It's becoming aware of and identifying when you are engaging in unwanted behavior or letting your fears control you and stopping yourself in your tracks. If you can recognize when it's happening, you can decide how you want things to go at that moment. This involves slowing down from our typical warp speed and becoming more present and less on autopilot. For example, let's just say I'm an overwhelmed mom of an infant running on no sleep. My mom wants to do me a favor and run out to the store for me to get baby wipes for my son because she knows I'm running low and will need more by tomorrow. She tells me she'll stop at the store on her way to my house to pick them up and, as much as I feel that would be extremely helpful; I decline. Why? Because as soon as I thought about it, another thought popped into my head; the possibility of her getting into a car accident on the way to or from the store and it being my fault that it happened because she was helping me. The instant reaction my brain has is to take away the situation completely and eliminate the possibility. Is it successful in preventing a make believe accident that took place in my head? Yes. Is it helpful? No. Especially since the store is only a few minutes from my house and is not out of the way for her. At the time, I may not have been aware of how I let my catastrophic thinking control my decision because I was so consumed by it, but now that I am aware of when this happens, I can take control back. I could do this by acknowledging the fear and saying to myself, "Yes, that is a possibility that could happen, but it's not likely to happen." Although anything is possible, because of all the factors that play into this (the store not being far, the time it would take her to go in and get the baby wipes, the time she would spend on a busy road, etc.) the odds are in my favor. If an accident did occur, although I may feel differently at the time, the reality is that helping me is ultimately her choice. Just how I make my own choices in life, so does she. I'm now giving myself time to acknowledge the fear, take it into consideration, and think it through before deciding. I can now accept the help she wants to provide me if I need it because I have said no to letting fear dictate me and have talked myself through my fear rationally.

Most of the time, fears are justified, but we may not think them through all the way because our view is unclear. It's kind of like we are looking through a dirty pair of sunglasses without wiping them clean. So in order to stop yourself in your tracks and give yourself time to wipe off those sunglasses, you need to realize when they are dirty and when you are not seeing clearly. It's OK if you put them on and then notice they are dirty (aka having the fear come up), but it's not OK to not take them off and clean them. In not taking action, we are keeping them dirty, therefore not seeing clearly, and then not moving because you are too afraid to trip and fall. Now that you're knowing you need to be more aware, the likelihood of you being aware of when this comes up and when it's controlling you is going to increase because I've brought it to your attention. It also might be helpful to note times in the past where this has happened (where you let fear and anxiety take control and dictate your decisions, actions, or lack thereof) and look for patterns. Maybe it's around certain people or activities for whatever reason...but noticing these things will help your brain to recognize and prepare for it. Awareness is seriously the first and most important step in the process of reclaiming control. You can use this with anything. Maybe it's not catastrophic thinking like the example I shared earlier. Maybe it's more along the lines of limiting beliefs or caring about what everyone else thinks. Or maybe it's striving to do things perfectly. Whatever is not serving you, shine a light on it, but more specifically on how you are letting it get in your way. Once you see how you are letting it get in the way and become aware of how you have the ability to change it.... Boom! There it is-the ball is suddenly back in your court!

"If you risk nothing, then you risk everything."

GEENA DAVIS

CHAPTER 2
JOIN THE CLUB

OK, so here is the part where I tell you that even though you may experience fear and anxiety, you're not crazy. You aren't. The problem with anxiety and fear is that everyone experiences them, but to different extents and although everyone does, not everyone talks about it. For example, for a long time, I thought that my catastrophic thinking and being able to picture something downright awful happening to someone I love was the equivalent of being a royally effed up person. How could I even imagine such a thing? What is wrong with me? No one else I knew had ever mentioned they've experienced anything like that, and I sure as hell wasn't going to talk about it. Then a few months ago, as I was watching a special on TV, there was a moment when a well-known speaker asked other moms in the audience how many of them have pictured something terrible happening to their kid when things are going great because of living from a "waiting for the other shoe to drop" mentality. At that moment I realized "Oh wow, this is a mind frame, and not that I'm an awful human being." I had a light bulb moment where I realized this may be more normal than I thought, and of course people are not super vocal about it, but when someone was, wow did it help me! When I truly acknowledge that something is amazing or that I am happy, I instantly get scared that I'm going to lose it or something is going to go wrong. I'm waiting for that other shoe to drop. This causes me to then live in a place of fear (aka letting fear take control). What I learned from this is that I am someone who understands the value of the people I have in my life and I fear losing them, which is a completely normal feeling to have. Where it becomes something different is what you decide to do with that fear. Do you never let your kid leave your sight? Do you not let them have simple life experiences that you did in fear something may happen or do you let them live a normal life knowing that life itself is a risk but one you are willing to take for the sake of having a quality of life?

Certainly not everyone has such catastrophic thoughts enter their mind often. Maybe you're someone who is just afraid of what other people will think, so you refrain from doing something you want to do. Or maybe you are someone who struggles with perfectionism and holds yourself to impossible standards, therefore never living up to what you think you should be. The point is, we all have our shitty anxiety induced and provoking habits. We all worry about something, at some point, in our lives. That's not a bad thing. It's when the worry takes over and controls our actions. That's what we want to prevent from happening. Anxiety is fear wrapped up in a confusing little package and in this book, my goal is to unwrap that package, acknowledge that there's a reason for it, learn from it, and then toss it out when we don't need it. The brain thinks it's helpful, but the reality is it's that one gift in the white elephant exchange no one wants. So what can we do with it? We can say, "thanks but no thanks" and then carry on with our lives.

"To grow yourself, you must know yourself."

JOHN. C. MAXWELL

CHAPTER 3
MAKING SENSE OF IT ALL

So much of our present results from our past experiences, especially our childhood experiences. Whether or not we want to admit it, our childhood shapes who we are as adults. Now, before I go any further, I just want to say I feel extremely blessed as I had a wonderful childhood, but I recognize how some events from my childhood have influenced me and fed into the anxiety I have today. I am not blaming any of my family members for this, but I feel it necessary to share my experience to help you see the connection in order to have a better understanding of your own anxiety and fears. When we understand something and it makes sense to us, we can feel more in control of it.

One of my earliest memories must have been when I was about 3 years old. I was sitting at our kitchen table enjoying my bowl of Cheerios when I heard a loud thump. I looked over towards the stairway and saw my mom laying at the bottom of the steps with the basket of laundry she had been carrying. Instead of picking herself up and brushing herself off, she lay there unconscious with the diet drink she had been living off of spilling out of her mouth and onto the floor. My brother and I ran over to her side and I just remember screaming at the sight. I sat there begging her to wake up. I remember thinking she was dead. My brother tried to wake her but couldn't. He then did something I'll never forget. He took the box of Cheerios from the kitchen table and started pouring them all over the floor. I don't know if he did this out of frustration or if he thought she would wake up and reprimand him for it. Either way, you can't blame a 5-year-old for reacting that way. A couple of seconds later, he started running up the stairs to get to the emergency button my parents had told us about in which they kept in their bedside drawer. When he reached the top of the stairs, her eyes opened, and she came to. She suffered a concussion and some neck issues, but no serious injuries. Until this day, when asked about it, she still says she remembers nothing, but waking up on the floor. My brother and I, however, are scarred for life. For the rest of our childhood and to this day, we both have always and still continue to experience an overwhelming amount of anxiety about her safety and well-being at all times. As a kid, I remember I would try to make deals with God to keep her safe. My brother ended up seeing a child therapist because he would panic every time she had to cross a nearby bridge in fear something would happen to her. Now we just have her location shared on our phones. This happens a lot, though. People sometimes have a traumatizing experience and don't realize how much it impacts them daily, even years down the road.

I love my parents and I think they did an amazing job

raising my brother and I. I also think that despite how well they did, they unknowingly instilled a sense of anxiety into us from an early age. I don't blame them for it. They were born and raised in Brooklyn, NY. They grew up extremely street smart, yet very weary at the same time. The Son of Sam was arrested blocks away from where they hung out, my great grandfather was mugged down the street from his house, and they grew up on the stoops and saw way more than I did. They were city kids, and they took the city with them when they moved to the suburbs. They taught us general safety such as never to take candy or get in a car with a stranger and all the basics, but it went even further, maybe a little over the top for a NJ suburb at that time.

As a kid, my mom would use phrases such as "lock all doors, man all forts," when telling us to lock the front door behind us or lock the car doors when we were inside. Seems harmless and was quite fun as a kid, but when you think about it, she was comparing our safety to being in the armed forces defending ourselves or our home from possible enemies. I remember when I was in my early twenties I went over to my friend's house whose parents were away and upon arriving found the door unlocked. I walked inside, only to hear the shower running. I remember reprimanding my friend for leaving the door unlocked when she was showering. I didn't watch a ton of scary movies, but I knew the shower scene to be a popular one, and I remember her laughing at me like I was talking crazy. Like a lot of people in the sub-urbs at that time, leaving the door unlocked was normal, but not for our family. That was considered dangerous to us.

When I was a teenager and I started driving, my par-ents enabled my fear of driving on the throughway for years because they also felt safer without me using it. It may have calmed their nerves, but it prevented me from getting anywhere I needed to go that was further away. I took the back roads almost everywhere for years. Any time I had to take the parkway, I ended up being a bun-dle of nerves until I had no choice but to consistently face my fear and use it to get to work every day.

My father was always concerned for his daughter's safety as any father would be, but he went as far as tell-ing me to look around and even underneath my car be-fore getting in it anytime I was in a parking lot. Don't get me wrong, I appreciate him telling me this; it helped me become more aware of my surroundings which is a good thing. However, reality is, as a young woman, it's a fright-ening thought having to look under your car every time you get in it in fear someone might be waiting to snatch you up. This sort of wearisome behavior wasn't just for me. If there was a strange car parked on our block, we'd get the license plate number just in case. There was even one time my father followed someone, who had been parked on our block, out of the neighborhood because he didn't like that they were parked by our bus stop.

These are just some of the many ways we grew up to be suspicious and weary of different situations. Again, I don't blame them for this. When I became a parent, I realized that you could be the best parent in the world and still mess your kids up one way or another. They did what they felt they needed to do to keep us safe and I appreciate that because it worked. Honestly, I'd probably screw my kids up in the same way if it keeps them out of harm's way.

Then there's the deeper stuff that trickles down from generation to generation and can impact how you think on a deeper level. My mom grew up a first generation Italian American with parents who loved her and her siblings very much, but also put a lot of value on how things looked to an outsider. It is important to note that they passed down amazing traditions, fantastic memories, and a lot of love, but I can't ignore that there was also a preoccupation with the question "what are people going to think?" As a teenager I remember visiting my grandparents in Florida and getting ready to go to church with them. My hair was scrunched at the time, as was the trend, and I remember my grandma passing me in the hallway and looking in disapproval. She stopped at the door and said "Go brush your hair... you can't go out like that...how will it look?" Several years later, every Friday or Saturday night as I was getting ready to go out with friends I recall my mother looking at my choice of clothing with disdain saying "What are people going to say about me, as your mother, if I let you go out like that?" I can assure you that on a promiscuous wardrobe scale of 1 to 10, I never reached a 5. I can understand and agree with a mother worrying about her daughter receiving negative attention, however more often than not it seemed to be accompanied by an underlying focus of what people will think of her. I always found it interesting because if you know my mother you would agree that she is one of the warmest, selfless human beings on the planet. It was obvious to me that this was a subconscious worry that had been passed down without her even realizing it. Would this happen to me too? Part of it is natural to think like that, but I also know that it's not healthy to be focusing on it. I can't help but think that it somehow has impacted my own unhealthy preoccupation with what I look like to other people. My grandma struggles with it, my mom struggles with it, and now so do I.

My early to mid-twenties were filled with love and heartbreak and just like many other people, I experienced the ups and downs of it all. Your relationships with others, whether they be family, friendships, or love interests, can impact the way you think as well. For me, the general feeling that came out of it which developed into a complex was "not being enough." I, without a doubt, brought some fun little baggage into my relationship for my now husband to deal with that he doesn't deserve, as he always makes me feel as though I am enough. Again, these are just some examples of how anxiety doesn't just pop out of thin air. It's learned behavior, fed by fear; fear of the unknown, fear of rejection or abandonment, or fear of not living up to either your own or some else's standards.

Take some time to think about your own anxiety, your own fears. Can you connect them back to your past? I bet if you take some time you can see why and how these inner beliefs, these worries or preoccupations came about. If you are a trauma victim or if the idea of thinking back to an event or your childhood, in general, is a triggering thought, this may be something you are not comfortable with or may trigger you further. If that's the case, I recommend skipping it or talking about it with a counselor or therapist.

I want to reiterate that this is not a blame game. I am not telling you to blame your parents or whomever in your life is connected to some circumstances that you feel contributed to your anxiety, unless of course you were the victim of a trauma, as that is different. For those of you who, like myself, have been impacted by occurrences or ideas but not victimized, I do not encourage you to harp on the past, as that is not the intention of this chapter. I wrote this to show how you can acknowledge, gain understanding, and learn about yourself. Once you do that, you can give yourself permission to move on from it. Your past will help you gain an understanding of why you may act or think certain ways, but it does not define who you are. You can choose what you want to keep and what you want to change. Understanding ourselves and how/why we function a certain way, helps us to make changes on a deeper level with more successful results.

"Change your story, change your life. Divorce the story of limitation, and marry the story of the truth and everything changes."

TONY ROBBINS

CHAPTER 4
FEEDING THE FEAR

My husband constantly reminds me of how I automatically always jump to the worst-case scenario. He doesn't understand how I think like that while I look at him in disbelief and think, "How can you not think about that? But he doesn't. What enters my brain in a flood of panic doesn't even cross his as an option, and for that I am extremely jealous. Mostly, he helps keep me grounded, but sometimes he is so relaxed about something that I end up turning into a control freak because I don't trust that he takes a situation seriously enough to make my nervous brain feel more relaxed. An example and one that I am even embarrassed to share is when we walk our dogs together. I always worry that he's holding our one dog's leash too loosely, which would allow for him to break free if let's say someone on a bike passed us (he hates bikes), or if he tugs on his leash from the front, which could cause the dog to come out of his harness by accident. Now is my fear unjustified? No. My dog has gotten loose a few times, and it's resulted in a wild goose chase in the past, but the likelihood of this happening is not high. The reality is my husband loves that dog just as much as I do. I know he would do his best to protect him from harm's way, therefore I need to trust him more with our dog's safety instead of annoying the shit out of him with my persistent reminders on how to safely walk a dog.

But when it comes down to it, it's what you tell yourself that's feeding the fear. If you walk around thinking, I can't trust anyone with anything, then you're not going to. If you think you're not good enough, then you will start noticing everything in your life that backs that belief instead of the one-hundred million things that back up the latter belief; that you are enough. What you focus on expands. An exercise I encourage you to try is to pick an unhelpful belief and tell yourself the opposite. Write it down, say it out loud, put it on your screen saver, ingrain it into your brain until you believe it. What you will notice is that once you focus on this positive belief, you will notice more of that in your life. For example, maybe you are single and haven't met the right person yet. You start to harp on the idea that maybe just because you haven't met someone yet, you will be alone forever because for whatever reason you must be unlovable. You start taking notice of all your friends who are in relationships, or how many wedding invitations you received this past year. You click on the TV and *He's Just Not That Into You* is on, and you start feeling lonely as you make yourself dinner and wallow in your own sadness. What would happen though if we cut that narrative and flipped the switch? What if we switched the belief to "I am never alone in life, I am surrounded by those who love and support me, and I am extremely worthy and deserving of love." What if we drill that into our brains instead? You will start to take notice of the support you received from someone at work today, or how many people went out of their way to wish you a Happy Birthday, or your dog or cat who cuddles up on your lap as soon as you sit down on the couch. Maybe you'll notice more opportunities for you to meet new people, and you'll put yourself out there more because you feel more confident because you know and truly believe you are a catch. Let's face it, confidence is sexy. What we focus on expands. If we deliberately start choosing a better belief, one that contradicts the basis of our fears-imagine the possibilities.

Let's stop and take a second now to think about and assess just how much our worries and fearful thoughts impact our lives. Notice all the times we overthink, worry about things we know are silly, or hold ourselves back because of our fears. It's pretty eye-opening. Here we are thinking it doesn't impact our day to day, but it does. Maybe not in the "I can't leave the house" or "I need to talk to someone right now" kind of way, but little by little the choices you make that are impacted by your fears can eventually change the direction of your life. This is why it is so important to get a handle on it now. It can stop you from pursuing your dreams, impact your relationships, leave you with feelings of depression and sadness, exhausted, physically unhealthy and even impact your long-term health.

Many people think that big changes need to be made in order to transform one's life. What they don't realize is that it's the small, very manageable and doable steps or actions when taken on a consistent basis that make the biggest impact. If you are thinking, "Oh crap... I have work to do," you don't need to be overwhelmed. Throughout the remainder of this book, I will provide you with small simple changes you can make that can help you feel more in control, and take back what's yours! Will they make your anxieties disappear? It's possible but I'm not guaranteeing it. It's difficult to fully unroot a behavior that was cemented in from childhood or years of experience. What I can promise is that if you try to implement what I share with you, you'll start to notice that these thoughts and fears will have less of an impact on your life, behaviors, and choices. You will know how to handle them when they come, and how to say, "No thanks, I'm good," instead of entertaining them.

"Nothing can bring you peace but yourself."

RALPH WALDO EMERSON

CHAPTER 5
THE LIGHT BULB MOMENT

I'll never forget the day it all clicked for me. I was sitting in on a free virtual training I had signed up for and the coach was talking about how, in order to overcome our fears, we have to first acknowledge them and their purpose. This is the part that blew my mind because it's actually so simple that it's silly. Anxiety is a fear of the unknown. That's it...-that's all it is. Fear has a function, to keep us safe. Anytime you fear something, it is your brain saying, "Wait a second...this is new and different. This is unfamiliar! Danger! Danger!" Now that might be a bit dramatic but what it's trying to do is keep you safe, even if there is no known physical harm. It can sound the alarm at any situation that feels unfamiliar, risky, or has the potential to make you feel uncomfortable. You might be thinking, well that's a good thing because I don't want to get hurt or be uncomfortable. Yes, sometimes it keeps us out of harm's way (clear danger) and other times it's keeping us from doing something that will end up helping us in the end because remember, growth takes place outside of your comfort zone. Fear is our brain's way of keeping us in status quo where everything is predictable and safe without risks. Sometimes, our brain is correct in making us feel fear, and other times, it's more like your super overprotective grandmother who worries about everything. Our job is to decipher the real danger versus living and experiencing what you want. Everyone knows someone (or maybe it's you) who lives life in a very calculated risk free fashion. That's all good and safe, but sometimes we need to take risks in order to achieve the goals and aspirations we have for ourselves. By risk, I don't mean life threatening, I mean putting ourselves out there to feel uncomfortable. There's a difference between running across several lanes of traffic when the light is green versus public speaking. One poses a risk of death and the other maybe a red face and forgetting your lines, but not death-you get the picture. Once you put yourself out there and do that presentation in front of an audience of people, even if your face is red and you think everyone thinks you're an idiot, chances are your fear has now somewhat diminished because you survived it and you didn't die. Maybe you impressed everyone in the audience or maybe you didn't, but even if you impacted just one person in the entire room (perhaps even by your courage to put yourself out there), well that makes the entire experience a success. Either way, none of it would have happened if you stayed small and didn't show up for yourself out of fear.

So when we understand that fear is trying to help us, we can accept it, and then choose a different path. We acknowledge it, thank our brain for trying to keep us safe, and then we decide on what we want to do next, and that decision is based on our intuition. Now this is where I used to get tripped up because my brain had presented me with so much anxiety and fear in the past that I wasn't sure if I could trust it and so I would end up questioning whether it was my intuition talking, or my ego. Your ego speaks to you out of fear and judgement, while your intuition speaks to you from a place of love. You can feel when you are being led by your intuition because it's a more of a calm feeling of certainty that you can feel in your body.

You don't need to decide whether or not your brain is working against you. It's working for you all the time because it wants you to stay safe. It just doesn't understand the complete picture, so you can do yourself a favor and scratch trying to figure that part out. You can, however, let yourself feel into decisions to get an idea if your ego or your intuition is guiding you. I had thought my ego was my enemy, therefore I was trying to ignore it instead of acknowledge it. What happens when you ignore an elephant in the room? You end up realizing that you can't because it will never go away. If we simply acknowledge it, say thank you for caring and then let it go, we can free ourselves of its peskiness. When this process sunk in, it was like a light bulb had finally gone on in my head and when I tried it, I felt free from the chains of my own fears. I'm not going to tell you this was the very first time I had heard of all of this because throughout the years I had learned pieces of it, but it all seemed to come together on this day. It's as if I had the directions in the form of a puzzle and had been missing that last puzzle piece, and it now felt complete!

What I want to drive home, though, is that anxiety has a purpose, and when we acknowledge that and understand it, suddenly it becomes a lot less scary. It doesn't necessarily go away and no matter how hard you try you can always find something to worry about. If you search for it, it will always be there. But you don't have to search for it, you don't have to give it weight, and you can choose to simply acknowledge its presence, and say, "No, thank you."

" You have to train your mind like you train your body."

BRUCE JENNER

CHAPTER 6
CREATING A TOOLBOX

Now that we understand our own anxiety and fears, how they came about, and what we do that feeds into them, let's talk about how we can get our control back and for good. I've already shared a little of what has worked for me and the basics behind it, but now I'd like to share with you my personal tool box to see if there is anything in it that will help you. The idea behind these next few chapters is to let you in on everything I've learned in my personal journey that can help you take back control of your fears and anxiety. I encourage you to try them out for size and see what works best for you. Then you can fill your own toolbox and pass it on to someone else who can benefit from this.

TOOL #1: ACKNOWLEDGE, ACCEPT, LET IT PASS

This first method is one I've already shared with you; however I'll break it down further. It's a 3-step process that must be done together. If you don't plan on doing all three, then I suggest not doing it at all because they only work when done together. Let it sit (or in other words acknowledge it). Accept it. Let it pass. What does this all mean? Let it sit basically means when you are experiencing a fear or an anxious thought, don't ignore it. Instead, welcome it, but let's also not get carried away when I say this. Welcome it, but not with open arms and don't invite it to stay for coffee! What I mean by this is to acknowledge it without turning it away. The reason for this is if we don't acknowledge it, it's going to be like that annoying little brother or sister that keeps pestering you until you pay them attention. Give it attention now so it doesn't keep coming back. To be clear, I'll repeat the steps. You are going to acknowledge the fear exists, then you accept it which means you say, "OK I hear you, I understand the message or in other words how you are trying to protect me... Thank you for caring." This also includes noticing your own reaction to it, how your body is reacting. Maybe your heart is racing. Maybe you have a headache. Maybe you are feeling flustered. Do yourself a favor and check in with yourself for a minute. Take a few deep breaths or whatever you have to do to calm yourself down and get back into a controlled state. Slowing down and becoming present in the moment allows us to stop and think through it logically. We say, "OK thank you, we understand your concern," check in with ourselves and return to a calm and controlled state, and then think through it to determine if there is in fact a real life-threatening risk, or if our brain is just being overly cautious and protective. If it's a life-threatening risk, then we listen to it and do what needs to be done. However, if it is our brain just being over protective, we can let it go. Letting it go means you made your peace, and you made a decision to not hold on to it anymore. We are not storing it away for later, we are not accepting it as truth (unless it in fact was a dangerous threat), and we will not continue thinking about it. We make a calm and conscious decision to let it go and we release it so it doesn't stay with us anymore. Now, if you feel you need to do something physical to release it, you can take a deep breath and release it slowly, blowing the air out and with it your worry. You can stretch or do a power pose to show your body is not holding on to anything, or you can make a motion that feels good to you and represents letting go.

Most of the time, we do one of two things. We either ignore our anxiety until it gets to an overwhelming level and causes us to have an attack or we invite it in for coffee and entertain it for hours without letting it back out. When we take the time to both acknowledge it, make sense of it, rationally make our own decisions, and then push it out the door for good, we are not pushing against a growing force or holding on to something that doesn't belong. We are letting it easily flow through on our own terms. Each action has a specific purpose that serves us for a limited period, and when we follow this, we own the process instead of the emotions and feelings owning us.

TOOL #2: REPLAY THE SCENE

This one is more for those catastrophic thoughts that pop into your head or if you always think of the worst-case scenario playing out. When it occurs you say, "OK, thanks but no thanks, I'm going to replay the scene." Pretend you are a director and you just saw a scene play out where you don't like the ending. It's just not sitting well with you and you can't possibly let it go to film like that so you say, "CUT!" You start it over, but change the ending to the best-case scenario or one that brings you more peace. In this exercise we are choosing not to accept that disagreeable movie scene. It doesn't serve us, so we don't entertain it. Remember not to be hard on yourself for these scenes playing out in the first place. Please don't be like me and start thinking there's something deeply wrong with you for imagining these things because there is nothing, and I repeat NOTHING wrong with you. Your brain is playing out this scene because it's trying to keep you safe (even if it's not about you). For example, I may worry about something bad happening to my child, but that's my brain trying to protect my heart because it knows I love and deeply care about my child (or whomever I am worried about). This is not serving me at the moment and I know that, so I am replaying the scenario back in my head until I feel better about it. You must replay it back from start to finish in order for this to be effective. By doing this, you are correcting your brain and teaching it who's boss. It may come up with its own movie scenes, but you call the shots on what stays and what goes.

TOOL #3: UNDERSTANDING WHAT YOU CAN CONTROL AND WHAT YOU CANNOT.

Most people worry about things that are out of their control. Even though it's human nature, it's kind of silly when you think about it because most of the time there's not too much we can do about it. I remember talking to my old therapist about all the things I worry about regarding my mom's actions and safety (remember I shared my over protective nature of her since watching her lay unconscious in front of me as a child). My therapist looked at me and said, "I understand, but your mom is a grown woman who knows how to take care of herself and you cannot control her. You can only control your own actions and your reactions, so there is no point in worrying about everything she is doing. You need to trust that she can make her own decisions and let her live her life. You cannot dictate or live her life for her." As harsh as it sounds, she is right. I think it is necessary that we are reminded of this throughout our lives. Reminded of what we can control, and what we cannot. If we cannot control something or how it turns out, there is no point in worrying about it. From that point on, I started focusing on controlling my own actions and what I say to my mom, but that's where it ends. Because she is going to make her own decisions for her life, not me. I can only control my reaction to them. This has helped me tremendously. When a thought enters my head or I dip back into my old ways of worrying about another person's actions, I remind myself that I don't have control of that other person. They are grown adults and I have to trust that they will make the right choices for themselves. When you genuinely adopt this way of thinking, you will feel as if a weight has been lifted from your shoulders, allowing you to relax and breathe with more ease.

TOOL #4: LET GO AND LET GOD.

Sometimes we have to rely on our faith to get us through. Faith in God, faith in the universe, faith in a higher power. Let's face it, as advanced as we are as human beings, we just can't figure it all out in life. Sometimes it helps to leave it up to God and trust that He will handle it in one way shape or form. Maybe He will show us the way, provide us with a sign or a person in our life who can help us, or maybe we will get a full on miracle. Now I realize this process is easier for some than others, but I can tell you that if you believe, and truly trust; it works. If you ask for a sign and truly believe that you will receive and keep your eyes open for one, you shall receive that sign. I say this because we are sent signs all the time, but don't realize it. When we develop and strengthen our mindset that God/the universe/a higher power has our backs and that everything happens for us and not to us, we experience amazing things.

TOOL #5: TURNING LEMONS INTO LEMONADE.

I will not sit here and tell you that the anxiety you have experienced is a positive thing. However, I will ask you if you have learned anything from it. Maybe it's a life lesson, an experience that you can share to help others, or an obstacle you overcame in which you learned something about yourself. When we can find meaning in an experience, we can make peace with it. When we are not overwhelmed with negative emotions, we can think more clearly and when we think more clearly, we can have more control over our thoughts and therefore our actions. See what I'm getting at? I could sit here and be angry about the fact that I have spent so many minutes of my precious life feeling anxious and worried or I can realize that this is part of my story. I can acknowledge that throughout it all, I have learned how to manage my anxiety and have more control over it. I am sharing what I have learned with you in the hopes that it can help and lighten your load as well, therefore I believe it's all for something.

TOOL #6: ANSWER THIS: WHAT STORY ARE YOU TELLING YOURSELF?

It may seem crazy, but we often tell ourselves a story we believe in our head (which most of the time is not true) and then we only see or think things that validate our story. I shared this one in Chapter 4, but I think it's worth repeating. If I believe that I'm never enough, when things don't go my way, I'm going to interpret that as validation of my belief. If my husband isn't very talkative because he's tired or doesn't feel good, I'm going to assume he's losing interest in me. When my boss schedules a meeting, I'm going to assume she wants to talk about my job performance. When I'm having a rough day and don't have any patience with my toddler because I'm exhausted, I'm going to think maybe I just don't have what it takes to be a good mom. We tend to make things about us even when they aren't. Think about all the times you internalized a situation and made it about you (even if it was just in your head) when it had nothing to do with you. Happens more than we'd like to admit, right?

The trick here is awareness again. If/when we catch ourselves entertaining a self sabotaging story, we can rewrite the story so that it is more accurate and is one that better serves us. We may realize that maybe it's our own writing that makes little sense, and we need an editor with a fresh pair of eyes to help us see that it is in fact skewed. When we take time to work on it and make corrections, we can then interpret things differently and our thoughts end up being more positive and less anxiety provoking. Sometimes, this takes us consulting with another person to help us see where our story is skewed and sometimes it can just be us walking away from the thought and coming back with a clean pair of glasses. What we focus on expands. If we think the world is against us, we are only going to focus on how bad everything is. If we believe that life is a gift and that everything is working for us, we will notice how fortunate we are. If we focus on something negative and stop ourselves half way, then we win. We flip the story and we flip our mindset. It's up to us to gain awareness of when we are doing this so we can take the necessary action to gain control back.

TOOL #7: KEEP ONLY WHAT SERVES YOU AND LET GO OF WHAT DOESN'T.

(THIS ONE PIGGY-BACKS OFF THE PREVIOUS TIP)

We can also add in putting up boundaries when needed to protect ourselves. When we were knee deep in the pandemic, I'm talking April and May of 2020, my brother would call me and talk about how bad things were. He would share stories of people dying and how bad it would be if my immunocompromised father, who was going through chemotherapy at the time, got the virus. I knew about this already because like the rest of the world, I watched the news and stayed in the know. I knew he was right about my father, but regardless I would tell him to stop, and that I didn't want to hear it. I wasn't trying to be naive, but I had reached a point where I could not continue to have these conversations anymore. I told him, "I know and I agree with you, but I can't participate in this because I can't live in this anxious state." I was visiting it every day, but I couldn't live there. I knew that if I stayed there and went that deep, I would soon start to suffer from depression, so my only lifeline was to not let myself get to that point. On the outside, I was a nervous wreck, but I had to choose what served me and what didn't. I had to draw a line to keep myself above water.

Sometimes, as much as others may not like it, you need to establish clear boundaries. When you find yourself teetering on the edge of falling deep and you know an action, conversation, or state of mind is only going to bring you more anxiety, do yourself a favor and draw a line in the sand. Set some boundaries for yourself and let go of what doesn't serve you. Call it selfish, if you will, but the reality is I wasn't only thinking of myself. I was thinking of my son who I needed to be there for, and if I didn't take care of myself, I couldn't be there for him. After several arguments, my brother and I came to an understanding and realized that we both cope with things in different ways, even when we agree.

Another way you can use boundaries to protect yourself is by eliminating things that make you feel bad. I dislike watching horror movies, sad movies, or movies where a pet dies. Why? Because they make me feel upset and frankly, I don't want or need the negative energy I feel when I watch them. My husband doesn't understand why I won't sit and watch some of these movies with him, but it's important to me to spend my time doing things that bring me joy. I make a clear decision to set boundaries where I feel I need to in order to live a happier life. I don't spend a lot of time watching or reading the news for the same reason.

TOOL #8: BE CONFIDENT IN YOUR ABILITY TO HANDLE IT.

Anxiety is all about worrying about a possible outcome that has not happened yet, right? What if we were to decide that we will not worry about it and that we are going to put our faith in a better outcome? You probably would say, "But what if the feared outcome or something just as bad happens?" Then you have to ask yourself what the likelihood of that happening is, and if it does happen, you have to believe that you will handle it the best way possible. It's having trust in your future self so that you can unburden your present self. If you sit here worrying about it happening and it doesn't happen, then you wasted a ton of time worrying for nothing. What if you said, "I will not hold on to this worry now, but I will deal with it the best way I can if it does happen in the future despite it being very unlikely?" If that's not enough, if it helps to think it through and it's a situation you can see yourself working through effectively, then work yourself through it and then let it go. The important part, however, is to trust in your own ability to be able to handle it in the future if needed. Think about all the things you have handled successfully in the past, or have coped with successfully no matter how hard it was. You have been through a lot, you are here, you survived whatever it was, and you will handle anything that comes your way to the best of your abilities.

TOOL #9: WRITE IT OUT.

One of the best things I have ever done to lessen my own fears and anxieties has been to write them out. Make a list of literally everything you are afraid of happening. This can be just your anxieties or it can be reasons that are stopping you from doing things you want to do, such as "I am afraid people will think I'm crazy." These thoughts and fears are dancing around in your head, taking up space, time, and your health, some of it unspoken and most likely never written. We are going to literally take them out of your head and transport them onto a piece of paper. Once it's out of your head and on paper, your brain is free from holding on to the bullshit it was polluted with and you will be in awe of how good it feels. Trust me.

TOOL #10: REMEMBER THAT NO ONE CARES.

This one is going to sound harsh and insensitive, but is actually liberating in a way. A lot of times, we are preoccupied with what we think other people are going to think. I recently confided in my coach about how, after taking some time off from promoting my coaching practice on social media, I felt that I had to explain it or come back with a bang for my followers. She said to me "You don't have to worry about it... you know why? No one cares...no one probably even noticed..." Ouch! But umm guess what? She's right! Most of the time the things we stress about, if you think about it, is us thinking that everyone else cares about the way we look or what we do. For some reason we believe they are sitting around talking and having strong opinions about us. Your family and close friends might, but that's probably about it. Sorry to burst your bubble, but that's the truth. So why on earth are you wasting your precious time and energy on those who couldn't give a rat's *you know what* about what you're doing? Instead, don't let your limiting beliefs get in the way because of fear, and do what it is you are meant to, inspiring the sh*t out of those people along the way. Now that they will pay attention to.

For free resources and more good tips and tricks in managing high function-ing anxiety, fears, or limiting beliefs, visit https://bit.ly/NoThanksImgood.

"You'll never change your life until you change something you do daily. The secret to your success is found in your daily routine."

JOHN C. MAXWELL

CHAPTER 7
SETTING YOURSELF UP FOR SUCCESS

There are a few other practices that can help you as you incorporate this new way of managing your anxiety. These are more of a "no matter what, every day exercises" you can do to help create a calmer, more controlled lifestyle. Making some or all of these a part of your daily or weekly routine can help you set yourself up for success.

DAILY REMINDERS

The first is to provide reminders for yourself, such as daily mantras, or setting alarms on your phone throughout the day with a message for yourself. You can do this manually and leave notes in your lunchbox like your mom did for you when you were a kid, you can make it the background of your phone or computer, leave sticky notes or quotes in places around your house or office or wherever you are daily. Basically do whatever feels most comfortable or fun for you. Get creative with it and put some genuine effort into taking care of yourself in this way. It may sound silly, but it is powerful. It could be anything from an affirmation card to a bracelet with a word or message, or maybe it's a sticky note on your bathroom mirror, but whatever it is, make it meaning-ful. I'm not talking about a random "live love laugh" sign that you like, but doesn't hit you in the gut with a "damn, that hit home" kind of feeling. It could be a mantra, a quote, or a reminder to breathe if you need it. Just make it something that you will look at and be like "oh yeah" and not breeze right by it without thinking.

DE-STRESS

Then there's the old stress relief methods, which are basically anything that helps you relieve stress in a healthy way. It could be something super simple like punching a pillow, blasting music and singing in your car, watching your favorite movie, getting in a good old cry, or meeting up with friends for a drink. Or it could be dancing, watching something so funny you can't stop laughing, spending time with people you love, snug-gling with your pets, or going for a walk outside. Some people get creative and artsy, some play an instrument, exercise, get massages, ... you get the point. Then there's mediation, yoga, running, or something like therapy. The point is to do something that helps you get by and helps your anxiety stay at what feels like a manageable level. The reason for this is because when we feel more stress, even if it's not from a direct anxious thought, we are more easily overwhelmed. The goal is to stay out of overwhelm and keep your head thinking rationally. You can try out different stress relief methods or maybe you know what works for you and just need to put it into action. All too often people will say things like, "well I don't have time for that." You're not alone, I've been guilty of that too. Sometimes, life gets crazy and we feel like we have no time, but I have a solution for you: make time! I know it can be annoying to hear, but it's totally possible. It's not always easy, but always possible and you are worth the effort after all.

STOP WAITING FOR PERFECTION

One thing I've learned is that if you wait for the perfect moment or time to do something, it will never come. Why? Because the perfect time doesn't exist. The perfectionist in me, and maybe you too, needs to stop waiting. If you like to paint, don't wait for the perfect time or space-paint, draw, work with what you have. I love to write, but working full time and having a toddler at home doesn't exactly allow me all the time to sit down and write. If it makes me feel good, I need to figure out when I can do it. I may not have the best setup, maybe I'm sitting on my bedroom floor locked in my room instead of sitting on a beach somewhere completely inspired, but I'm writing with the time and space I have. Sometimes, we need to let go of our perfectionist tendencies to allow us to take care of ourselves. I find it's when I let my self-care fall to the wayside that my anxiety comes out to play more. Think of it as a prescription for your mental well-being. The doctor, aka you, is telling yourself this will help so do it at a minimum this many times per week, and do it no matter what because it's the only way to feel your best. Make it a non-negotiable and let go of perfect circumstances.

I used to get so tripped up by the idea that everything had to be a certain way for me to do things... and then I became a mother. It took me a long time to wrap my head around the idea that if I wait for things to be a certain way, I'll be waiting forever. I'm at a place where I understand that what I'm given right now (as far as the little time I have or circumstances I'm dealt with) is what I got. Therefore I better accept it, enjoy it, and make the most of it. I would love to be like Carrie Bradshaw, pouring out thought provoking, witty advice onto my laptop as I sit in my quiet apartment in my stilettos and stylish outfits. But here I am cramming in writing in the half hour I have to myself between when the baby goes to sleep and my eyes start to feel heavy, not to mention barefoot in a pair of old sweatpants with 20% of my brain still working from a long day. But hey, this is what I have, so let me use it to the best of my abilities. Why? Because it helps me-plain and simple.

BE NICE TO YOURSELF

This leads me into the next practice you can engage

in to help manage anxiety. It's called practicing self-love. What I mean by this is to be your own best friend, your biggest supporter, accept yourself for who you are, and love yourself for it. If you mess up, be understanding and forgive yourself. If you trip up the stairs in front of a bunch of people and totally embarrass yourself, laugh at yourself and then let it go. You won't continue to worry about how everyone else sees you or what they think because you will know that you are, in fact, an amazing person and their opinions don't matter in the grand scheme of things.

BEING TRULY GRATEFUL

Another thing that has a similar but even more powerful effect is gratitude, and I mean genuine gratitude. When my father was diagnosed with pancreatic cancer almost two years ago and we weren't sure what to expect or if he would even be here now, it was the biggest eye-opener for me. Suddenly, none of the small shit that would have normally wedged its way in-between us mattered anymore. All that mattered was enjoying time together and making sure he knew just how important he is to me. It's amazing just how powerful a life and death situation changes things and puts literally everything into perspective. Suddenly, none of the small stuff that once mattered does anymore. Thankfully, God has blessed us with a full recovery, but the lesson will never go away. All the things that used to eat at me, the grudges and the hurt from years passed vanished and were replaced with love and acceptance. Gratitude for what we have in our lives, things or people that can get taken away in an instant, reminds us to focus on what matters and directs us away from that which doesn't, even if it once felt so significant.

CLEAR OUT THE CLUTTER

The next lifestyle practice I would encourage is to declutter. I look at this as clearing the clutter both in your head and physically. Don't believe that this helps? Try it. The physical act of letting go of what no longer serves you helps your mental state more than you realize. When you have a clear, clutter free space, there's more room to think clearly and allow more of the new and better to come into your life. Whenever I'm feeling stressed or even want to start up something new, I usually have a nice little decluttering session. I get rid of what I don't or will not use, or put it away for the future if need be. This helps me to be more prepared and put my energy into the things that I want more of in my life.

BEING ENOUGH

One change that has taken a lot of practice for me is allowing my imperfections to be enough. The one thing that makes everyone feel stuck and as though they are behind is also the one thing that drives insecurities, doubt, and distrust...perfectionism. Think about it. Most likely, many of the smaller things you worry about boil down to our need to be or do something perfectly and the stress that comes about from the fear of not living up to or performing to that expectation. We set our expectations almost to an impossible level to achieve and then end up freaking out because of it. What if we just say, "I'll do the best I can," understanding that we are not perfect and be OK with this. Sometimes, we just need to cut ourselves a break.

As a parent, I've realized that some days might run smoothly and some days are going to feel like a sh*t show. Some days, I'll be the mom that gets her work done, takes her kids out to the park, feeds her family a delicious home cooked meal, and has a clean house. Other days the best I'll be able to provide is the comfort and safety of staying home and watching Sesame Street in a messy house with some take out....and that's OK. Instead of feeling crappy about myself or allowing my brain to accuse myself of being a terrible mom, and run down a path of "my kids are going to hate me, other moms will talk about me, my husband will think less of me," and so on and so forth, I'll just say, "OK well you did what you could today. They are safe, they are fed, and they know they are loved, mission accomplished!" It may not be ideal, but it sure helps prevent the unnecessary mix of the self-pity party/stress fest that would surely take over my brain otherwise.

CONNECT TO A HIGHER POWER

Last but definitely not least, let's not forget to mention that which is greater. I believe it's so important to tap into your own spirituality, whatever and however that looks to you. This is how you connect to something greater than yourself, a higher power. Whether it be religion or your own special connection to God, the universe, or angels... just lean into it. Pray, meditate, connect. This is probably the most powerful, yet overlooked lifestyle practice for managing anxiety.

"Every moment is a fresh beginning."

T. S. ELIOT

CHAPTER 8
YOU'VE GOT IT, NOW USE IT

I can feel it coming on now. My heart is racing for no reason at all. Sometimes I can feel my hand or foot shake uncontrollably. Mentally I know I'm OK but I don't feel OK. It feels like a lack of control over my body and that feels scary. I know I'll be OK because I know it's just anxiety. I know me, at least that's what I'm telling myself while the worry is trying to convince me that maybe it's not what I think. My brain wonders if maybe there is something wrong with me. Maybe it's chest pains leading to a heart attack, or maybe there's a tumor in my chest like there was for the girl in one of the twenty-seven episodes I recently binged of Grey's Anatomy. Perhaps it's the beginning of a stroke. It could be anything, but I'm sticking to "I know myself and I've felt this before."

Now that I'm confident in my diagnosis, I am acknowledging this as a signal, telling me that I'm failing myself. Sounds a bit harsh, but it's true. I haven't been taking care of myself lately and I can't deny that. I think back to all the times I've thought about going for a walk, or a run, all the times I've swallowed my own overwhelming emotions instead of journaling. When was the last time I've even had a good cry? I can't even remember because I've been too concerned with preserving my eyelash extensions that I haven't even let myself tear up for more than a minute. The truth is, there have been plenty of signs telling me what I should do, and I know what to do because I know what works for me, but I have ignored those signs because life got in the way and now my body is screaming at me to do something about it. Somewhere between my expectations at work and taking care of my family, I've put my own needs aside and now my brain and body are sounding its alarm so loud that it's near impossible to ignore.

I know I have the power to calm myself and then make a change, to turn this around. I know this because I've done it in the past. I know that when I don't let the stress out; it ends up manifesting in my body as aches, pains, mood swings, sadness, indigestion, shortness of breath, and heart palpitations. So when I'm feeling shaky from this, I know I have to talk myself calm. I'll take a few deep slow breaths, remind myself that I am in control, and then I get to work on letting it out in a way that works for me. In this case, I opened my journal and started writing.

I share this experience with you to show you the importance of taking care of yourself daily, and also to remind you that no one is perfect, and even when we have a full toolbox, if we are not using it, it doesn't work. It takes consistency and practice in order to make these tools work for you. Reading about them is fine, but utilizing them is golden. And even so, sometimes we get thrown off our feet when life gets in the way. We are not always going to practice them daily, weekly, or even monthly, and that's when your body will sound its alarm. It's OK if this happens. Pick yourself up, dust yourself off, and get back to work. The key here is to know that you are not perfect, but you are most definitely in control and you have the power to calm yourself and feel good again.

The truth is we may not be able to control all of the experiences life hands us, and we may not be able to control when fear pops into our minds. We can however, control our actions, our reactions, what we choose to entertain, and what we choose to change. Everyone has fears, everyone has doubts, but what makes one successful is what they do with those fears. Do you completely ignore them until they get bigger and bigger to the point where you can't possibly ignore their presence? Do you feel them and then get consumed to where you stay stuck in non action in order to play it safe? Or do you feel the fear, and then do it anyway? You, my friend, have the power to decide.

If you found this book helpful, I invite you to visit https://bit.ly/NoThanksImgood and sign up to receive free resources to assist you on your journey of reclaiming your power and living a happier life.

ABOUT THE AUTHOR

Maria is both a Life and Wellness Coach, a wife, and a mother. She has certifications in both Life and Health Coaching, as well as a background and Master's Degree in Mental Health Counseling. As a coach, Maria helps her clients move past their fears in order to create and navigate through the necessary changes needed in order to live the life they desire. She firmly believes that life is a precious gift and should be spent doing what you love. Through her work, she aims to help others live a life of purpose and joy. She resides in New Jersey and enjoys spending time at the shore with family and friends as much as possible.

Made in United States
Orlando, FL
01 March 2022

15250658R00062